숫자들의 이야기

THE NUMBER STORY

SMALL BOOK ONE

ENGLISH - KOREAN

Numbers Teach Children Their Number Names

written and illustrated by

MISS ANNA

Early Reader Edition of *The Number Story 1*
Bronze Medal Winner, 2016 Wishing Shelf Book Award

Library of Congress Control Number: 2018902040

Names: Miss Anna, author.
Title: Number story : numbers teach children their number names / Miss Anna.
Description: Portland, OR: Lumpy Publishing, 2018.
Identifiers: ISBN 978-1-945977-12-1 | LCCN 2018902040
Summary: The pictures and rhymes present stories which introduce numbers 0-10.
Subjects: LCSH Numeration—English--Korean--Pictorial works--Juvenile literature. | BISAC JUVENILE NONFICTION /
Languages: English--Korean
Classification: LCC QA141.3 .M57 2018 | DDC 513—dc23

Publisher: Lumpy Publishing
Website: www.missannabooks.com
Email: missanna@missannabooks.com

Paperback: ISBN 978-1-945977-12-1
Printed in the U.S.A.   1 3 5 7 9 10 8 6 4 2

우리 숫자들도

이름이 있답니다.

It is very easy and a lot of fun!

알기 쉽고 재미있게 알려줄까요?

Say-along our little jingle

지금부터 숫자들의 신나는 이야기를

starting from Number One!

우리 같이 들어봐요!

1

ONE   looks like my one finger.

하나 ☆ 일은 내 손가락 하나

ONE!
하나! 일!

2
TWO   trails a tail.
둘 이는 긴 꼬리

A TAIL! 긴 꼬리!

3

THREE   has bumps.

셋 ☆ 삼은 울퉁불퉁

BUMPY!   울퉁불퉁!

4

FOUR carries a sail.

넷 사는 돛단배

4
돛을 달았네!
A SAIL!

5
FIVE   is a racing track.
다섯 ☆ 오는 경주로

VROOM
부릉!
1

6

SIX   curves like a snail.

여섯 ✩ 육은 달팽이

A SNAIL! 달팽이!

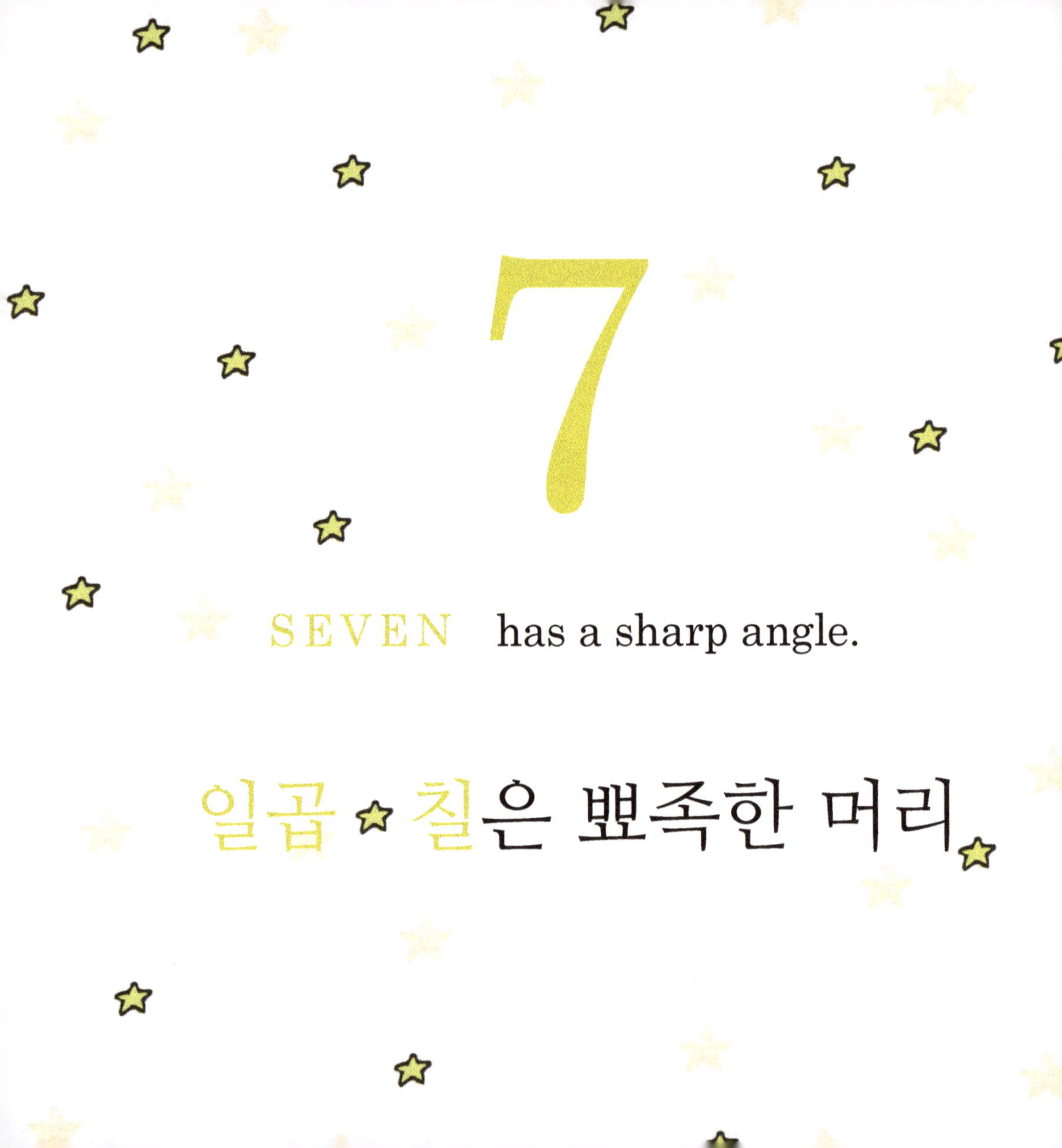

7

SEVEN has a sharp angle.

일곱 ⭐ 칠은 뾰족한 머리

OUCH!
아야!

8
EIGHT   is rollercoaster rails.
여덟 팔은 롤러코스터

야호!
YIPPEE!

9

NINE   is a bubble on a stick.

아홉  구는 버블 놀이

비눗 방울 놀이

A BUBBLE! 비눗방울

10

TEN is an eye of a whale.

열  십은 고래의 한쪽 눈

윙크!
WINK!
HELLO! 안녕!

And
그리고

0

ZERO   is an empty pail.

영 ✦ 공 ✦ 제로는 빈 깡통

IT'S
EMPTY!

비어있네!

Thank you for playing with us today.

We had a lot of fun too!

같이 놀이줘서 고마워요.

저희도 즐거웠답니다!

We are your Number friends,
Zero to Ten,
Who will be here for you~
우리 숫자들은 좋은 친구로
늘 옆에 있어줄께요~

Bye-bye now!
See you again soon.
곧 또 만나요. 안녕!

The Numbers are *SINGING* too!

To sing-a-long, look for Miss Anna Number Story
at your favorite music store like iTUNES.

MP3

Numbers 0-10
IDENTIFYING
& COUNTING

Numbers 11-20
& Ordinals

first, second, third…

Numbers 0-100
& Place Values

ones, tens, hundreds…

About Clocks
& Telling Time

hours, minutes, seconds

Number Story 1 & 2

isbn: 978-0-996216-48-7

Number Story 3 & 4

isbn: 978-1-945977-01-5

Number Story 5 & 6

isbn: 978-1-945977-06-0

Number Story 7 & 8

isbn: 978-1-949320-40-4

For more Miss Anna books to love,
visit us at

w w w . m i s s a n n a b o o k s . c o m

Numbers are working hard all over the world!
Come Travel the World with Us!

www.ingramcontent.com/pod-product-compliance
Lightning Source LLC
Chambersburg PA
CBHW040902070726
47599CB00035B/2277